WAYS INTO GEOGRAPHY

Using
Maps

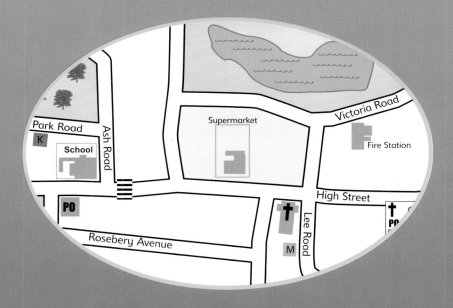

Claire Llewellyn

W

FRANKLIN WATTS

LONDON•SYDNEY

This edition 2012

First published in 2009 by
Franklin Watts
338 Euston Road
London NW1 3BH

Franklin Watts Australia
Level 17/207 Kent Street
Sydney NSW 2000

Series editor: Julia Bird
Art director: Jonathan Hair
Design: Shobha Mucha
Artwork: John Alston
Consultant: Sam Woodhouse, Associate Consultant for
Geography and Citizenship, Somerset

A CIP catalogue record for this book is available
from the British Library.

Dewey classification: 526

Picture credits:
Alamy: 7: (t) © Ilene MacDonald; 12: © James Jagger; 13: © The Photolibrary Wales; 16: ©
David Taylor; 22: © Robert Stainsforth; 24: (t) © Alex Segre. Istockphoto: 7: (b) © Gary Martin;
19: (bl) © Debi Bishop; 24: (b) © Mark Richardson; 26: (t) © Hubert Gruner; (b) © Guillermo
Garcia. Shutterstock: cover & 6 (t) © Jan Kranendonk; (b) © Marcin Balcercak; 11: © Pichugin
Dmitry; 27: © Ronald Sumners.

Every attempt has been made to clear copyright.
Should there be any inadvertent omission, please apply to
the publisher for rectification.

ISBN 978 1 4451 0954 1

Printed in China

Franklin Watts is a division of Hachette Children's Books,
an Hachette UK company.
www.hachette.co.uk

Contents

Maps help us

Maps are very useful.
They help us find our way around.

A street map helps tourists to find their way around a big city.

Walkers use a map to make sure they keep on the right path.

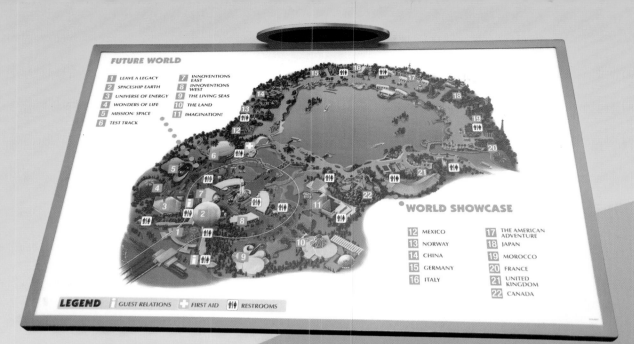

This map of an adventure park helps visitors to find the rides they like.

Drivers use road maps to plan their journey.

We need maps when we visit new places. What places might you visit where you need a map?

Looking at a farm

Kalem has a model farm.

There is a barn, a chicken coop,
a pig-sty and a sheep pen.

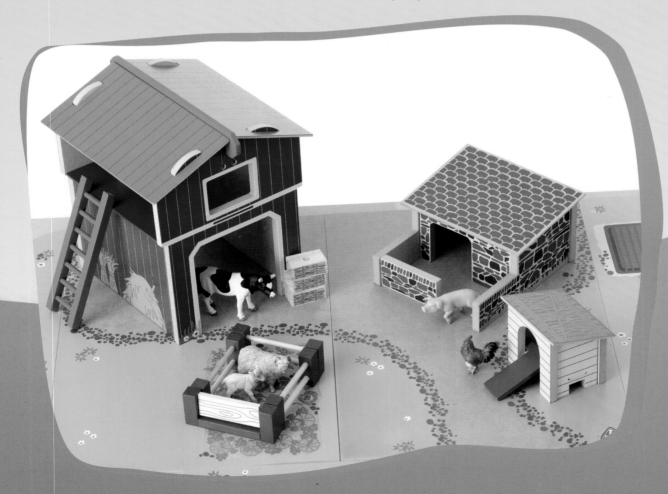

Kalem has added some hay
bales and some plastic animals.
Where has he put them?

Kalem gets some paper and pens.
He draws a picture of his farm.

How could Kalem turn his picture into
a map? Turn the page to find out.

A map of the farm

Kalem puts a big sheet of paper under his farm.

Then he draws around all the buildings.

That way, he knows they are in the right place.

On this drawing, the farm looks different.

This is how a bird would see it, high up in the sky.

It is called a bird's-eye view. Maps always show a bird's-eye view.

Can you tell what each shape in the drawing is meant to be? How could Kalem make it clearer?

Looking at a castle

This is a photo of a castle.

Can you see its grey walls?
Can you see some round towers?

This photo was taken by a person
standing on the ground.
It is a ground-level view.

Here is another photo of the castle.

It is called an aerial photo.
It gives a bird's-eye view.
Where do you think it was taken from?

What does the ground-level photo
show that the aerial photo doesn't?
What does the aerial photo show that
the ground-level photo doesn't?

Maps and symbols

Hannah has a map of the castle.
It gives a bird's-eye view.

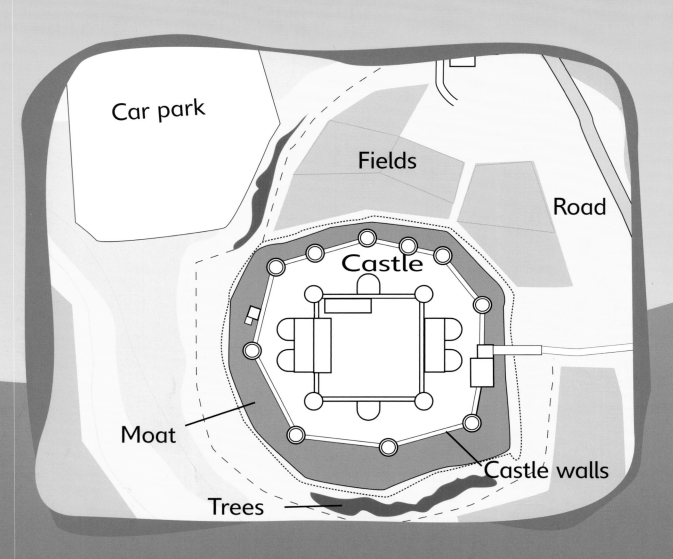

Some things on the map have been labelled.
Can you match these with the things you can
see in the aerial photo on page 13?

Hannah draws her own map of the castle.
Her map looks a little different.

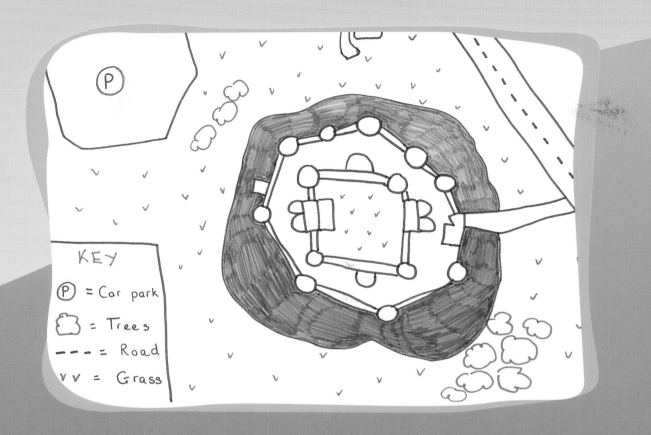

Instead of labelling the trees, she has
drawn a symbol. She has also drawn
a symbol for the car park.

Map symbols stand for things on the ground.
A key tells you what the symbols mean.

What other symbols can you see on Hannah's map?

How far is it?

Kalem has drawn a map of his school.

In real life, the school is big but this map is quite small.

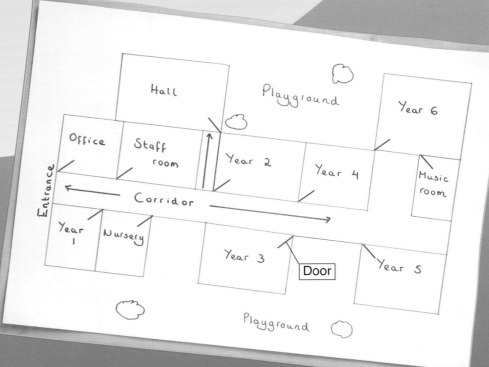

Maps help us to understand distance.

Kalem is in Year 3. He measures how far it is from his classroom to the hall. He uses his foot as a measure. It takes 40 foot-lengths to walk to the hall. That is about four centimetres on the map.

Next, Kalem measures the distance from his classroom to the Year 6 classroom. Using the map, can you estimate how many foot-lengths it takes?

Welcome to Reed

This is a map of a village called Reed. There are many different buildings and places in the village. Some of them are marked on the map.

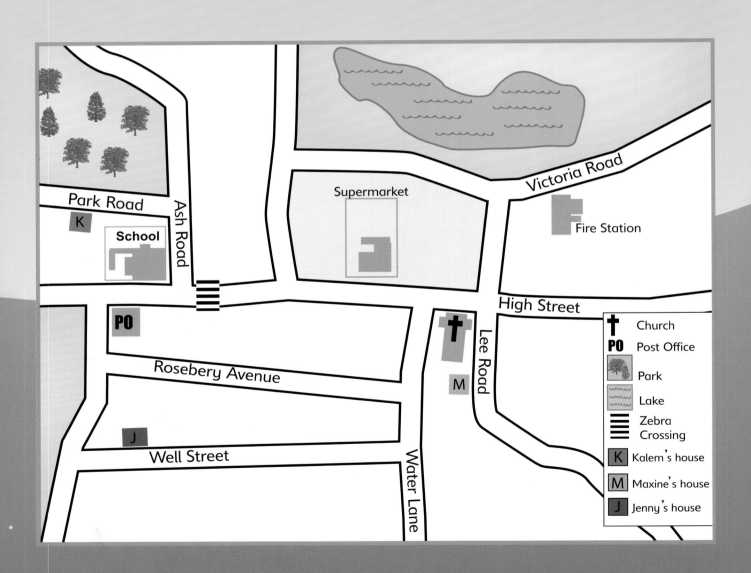

Can you find the church?
Can you find the lake?

What symbols have been used to draw them?
What other symbols can you see?

Kalem

Maxine

Jenny

Kalem, Maxine and Jenny all live in the village.
Who lives nearest to the school?
Who lives nearest to the church?

Finding the way

Kalem is having a birthday party.

His friend Maxine is new to the village. She will need a map to find the way. Kalem draws one for her.

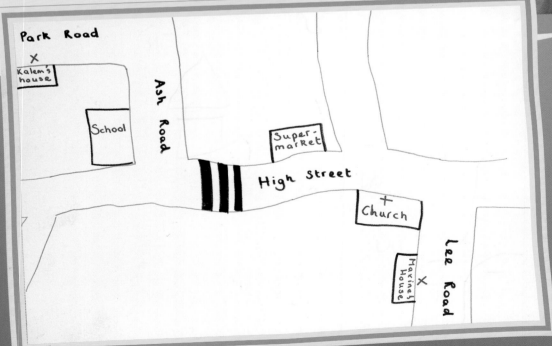

Maxine leaves her house and walks up Lee Road. She walks past the church and turns left into the High Street.

Next, Maxine crosses the road at the zebra crossing. She turns again at the school. Does she turn left or right?

She turns left when she reaches Park Road. Kalem's house is Number 3.

At the zoo

Matthew and his friends are visiting the zoo. They need a map to find their way around.

In the morning, the boys want to look at the reptile house, lions and giraffes, penguins and seals. Then they plan to have lunch in the café.

In the afternoon, they want to visit the petting zoo, flamingos and elephants.

Can you work out their route on the map?
Which other animals will they pass on the way?

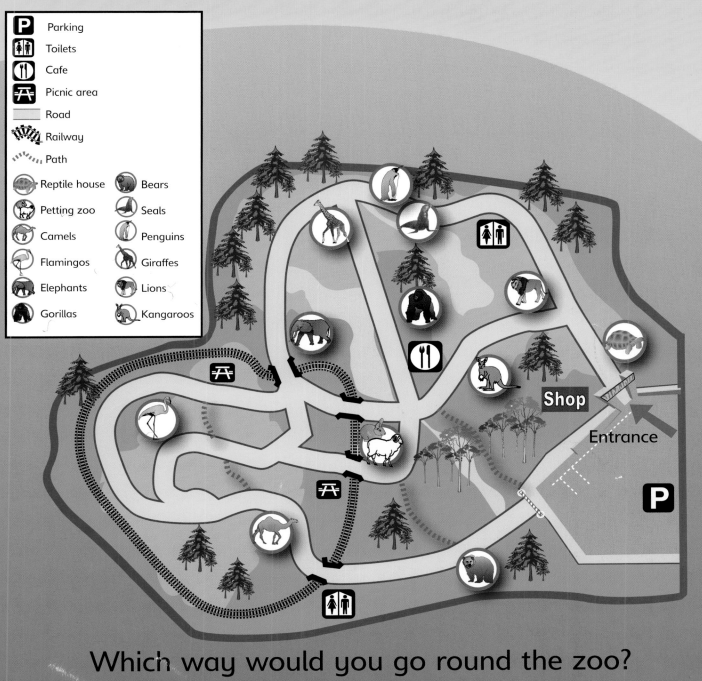

Which way would you go round the zoo?
Which animals would you like to see?

A day out

The Chapman family are on holiday at Sandy Bay.

They are planning a day out. Sophie and Lizzie want to take a boat trip to Black Rock Island.

Dad wants to visit Oak Tree Farm. Mum wants to visit the museum.

They look at a map of the area.

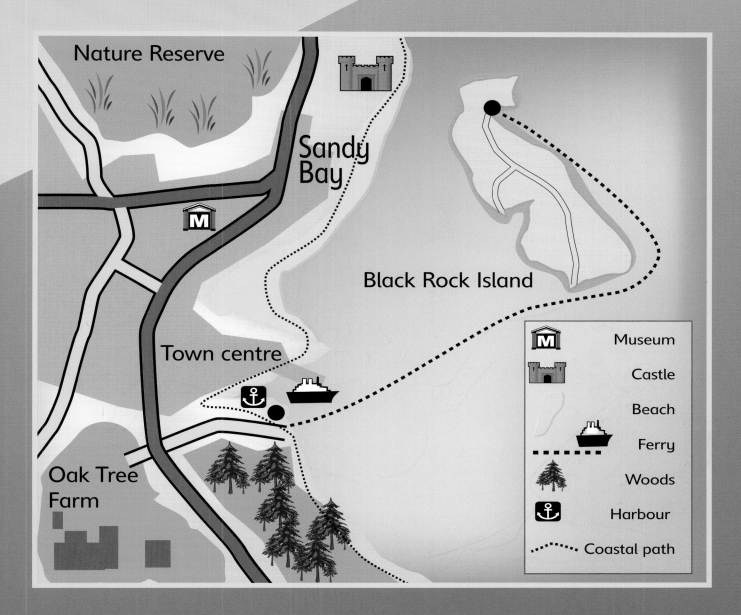

Nature Reserve

Sandy Bay

M

Black Rock Island

Town centre

Oak Tree Farm

M	Museum
	Castle
	Beach
	Ferry
	Woods
	Harbour
····	Coastal path

Can you find all the places on the map?
Look at the other places marked on the map.
Where would you choose to go?

Where in the world?

Alice and Sam are travelling around the world. They are visiting many different countries.

They send a postcard to their family when they arrive somewhere new.

This postcard came from India.

This postcard came from Australia.

These countries are marked on this map of the world. Can you find where you live on the map?

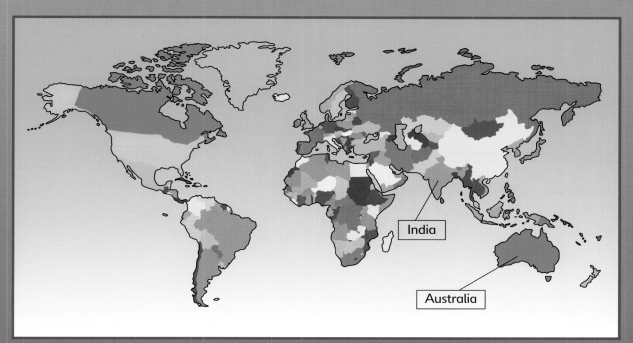

India

Australia

Useful words

Aerial – from the air.

Area – a part of the country.

Bird's-eye view – a view seen from high above.

Country – a place, such as India or France, with its own land and people.

Distance – how far it is from one place to another.

Ground-level – on or from the ground.

Journey – a long trip from one place to another.

Key – something that explains the symbols on a map.

Label – a word or two that explains something.

Measure – to find out how far away a place is.

Route – the way you plan to go from one place to another.

Symbol – a shape that is used on a map to stand for something on the ground.

Tourist – a person who visits a place for fun.

View – the way we see something from a particular place.

Some answers

Here are some answers to the questions we have asked in this book. Don't worry if you had different answers to ours; you may be right, too. Talk through your answers with other people and see if you can explain why they are right.

Page 7: There are lots of different answers to this question. You might need a map when you go to the seaside, visit a relative, or go to a friend's house for the first time.

Page 8: Kalem has put the haybales in front of the barn. The cow is in the barn. The pig is in the sty. The chicken is near the coop. The sheep are in the pen.

Page 11: Kalem could make the drawing clearer by adding labels to the shapes or colouring them in different colours.

Page 13: The picture has been taken from high up in the air.

Page 13: In the ground-level picture, you can see the hills behind the castle and some cows in front of the castle. In the aerial picture, you can see the whole shape of the castle. You can see the moat, the inner walls, the grass in the middle, the car park and the road.

Page 15: You can also see symbols for the road and for grass on Hannah's map.

Page 17: It is around 45 foot-lengths to the Year 6 classroom.

Page 19: The symbol of a cross has been used for the church. Blue shading has been used for the lake. Tree symbols have been used for the park, the letters PO for the post office, and black and white lines for the zebra crossing.

Page 19: Kalem lives nearest to the school. Maxine lives nearest to the church.

Page 21: Maxine turns right at the school.

Page 23: There are two possible routes. On one route, the boys will pass the kangaroos and the gorillas. On the other, they will only pass the gorillas.

Index

About this book

Ways into Geography is designed to encourage children to think about the local and wider world in a geographical way. This title, **Using Maps**, is a way in for children to begin to use maps and plans to identify and describe where places are and to plan a route. They will also use fieldwork skills, observing the world around them and finding out how it can be plotted on a map.

By working their way through this book, children will be learning the following **geographical skills**:

1. To use geographical vocabulary (National Curriculum 2a).

2. To make maps and plans (National Curriculum 2e).

3. To identify and describe where places are. (National Curriculum 3b).

Learning content

By using this book, children learn that there are different ways of viewing the world around us. They will begin to use geographical concepts such as features, distance and scale.

Previous work and resources

Children need to have plenty of practice using many different kinds of maps.

To extend the theme of viewpoint, children could look at a selection of photos of familiar places – some taken at ground level and others from the air. Can they match one with the other?

It might help the children's understanding of symbols and how and why they are used (so they are clear and can be understood by everyone, even if they cannot read or speak a different language) to look and compare symbols in everyday use – for example, along the road or on toilet doors.

The last spread is an extension activity that relates the topic to the wider world.